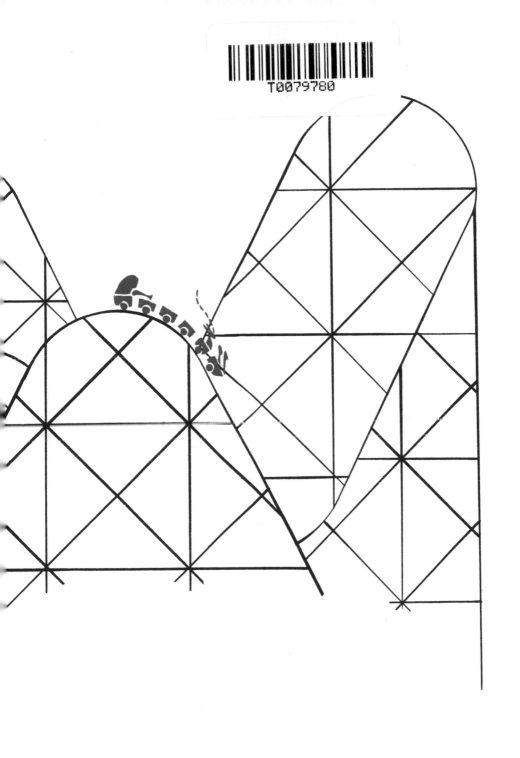

Albert Einstein's Bright Ideas

Albert Einstein's Bright Ideas

Narrated by
Frédéric Morlot

Illustrated by
Anne-Margot Ramstein

Translated by
Anna Street

Plato & Co.
diaphanes

4

On a rainy morning in the autumn of 1896, the only thing
that could have enticed the inhabitants of the city of Munich
to come outdoors was the opening of the famous Oktoberfest!
This beer festival was the city's major entertainment,
and since pastimes were becoming rarer as winter approached,
the fine people of Bavaria were eager to have a good time.

On the Theresienwiese—the fairgrounds where the festival
was held—the hustle and bustle was intense. Amidst the
hullabaloo of the fanfares and the hurdy-gurdies, the young
and the not-so-young were having a splendid time, their
stomachs full of grilled sausage and cinnamon buns.
The children were squealing on the carousel, the parents were
shrieking on the roller coasters, and the dogs were howling
at the sight of the bear tamer.

5

The innkeepers of the city had built big barns into which they crammed tables groaning under tankards of beer and food, surrounded by cheerful visitors. The morning had barely begun yet hearty singing had already broken out among the beer and pretzel lovers. Erected between the Ferris wheel, the photographer's stand and the bearded woman's booth, the Schottenhamel marquee was without a doubt the grandest of them all: it resembled an immense wooden chalet like the ones scattered across the Bavarian mountains, decorated with brightly-painted colors. Its size was legendary; people say that it was two hundred thousand miles long!

Schottenhamel, the owner, was a sort of potbellied goblin with
a red beard straight out of a Grimm fairytale. Rumor had it that
he was one of the richest men in Munich. With such a big marquee,
capable of accommodating two beer-drinkers every meter and
every hour, he had calculated that he could serve close to fifteen
million liters of beer per day. He had hired strong, matronly women
specially trained to carry up to five thousand steins with one hand.
But despite all their efforts, the average delay for being served was
one year and three days, which meant that one could find customers
there from last year still waiting. In short, a tavern as imposing as
this one required a very special decoration. And so Schottenhamel,
who was beginning to foster political ambitions, was proud to offer
a new display to his customers: the electric fairy show.

On this particular day, young Albert Einstein found himself at the fairgrounds because his uncle's company had been commissioned to install the electric lights for the show. He had brought his little sister Maja along. She was all spruced up, sporting leather pumps and her dirndl, the traditional Bavarian dress with pretty flowers. In a corner, next to a window, their dog Heinrich was dozing, a fiercely loyal dog who owed his name to a great German poet.

Unperturbed by the delicious aroma of the Putensauerbraten escaping from the kitchen, Albert and Maja conscientiously screwed in the last light bulbs of a great string of Christmas lights, intended to illuminate the entire room from the main entrance.

Schottenhamel had solemnly announced a light show to his customers for 10 o'clock, and he insisted that everything be ready on the dot. Knowing how important punctuality is to Germans, Albert and Maja were not fooling around but doing their very best to have everything finished in time, which was no small feat.

Finally, at exactly 10 o'clock, they flipped the switch, and the room lit up to a chorus of "ooohs" and "aaaahs" from the customers. Albert, Maja and Heinrich looked proudly upon their accomplishment when they noticed Schottenhamel coming towards them with long strides.

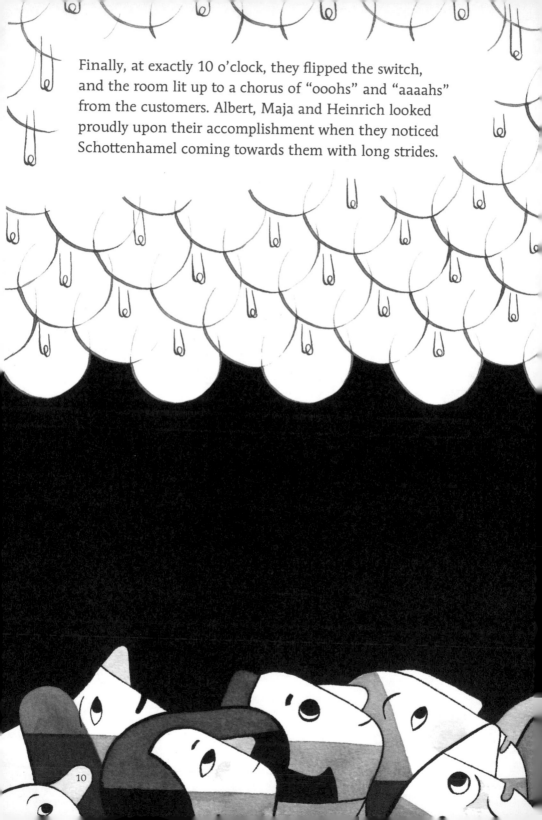

"What is the meaning of this, you little scoundrrrels? I asked you to light everrrything up at 10 o'clock, but you trrricked me! I was watching my watch frrrom the back of the rrroom, and it was one second past 10 o'clock when the lights came on. A second is a second, orrr my name is not Schottenhamel! This is unacceptable, what do I look like in frrront of my customerrrs?"

11

Feeling rather small and at a disadvantage, Albert timidly explained to the innkeeper:

"I'm not entirely sure, Mister, but I think I have an explanation; I learned in high school that light is not a completely instantaneous phenomenon. Even if light travels fast, it does not have infinite speed. In fact, your inn is so vast that it must take the light an entire second to pass through it."
"I understand nothing of your mutterrrings. Donnerrrwetterrr! Do whatever it takes, but I want all my customers to have light at the same time, for goodness' sake! I am giving you a second chance: in one hour, at precisely 11 o'clock, we will try again, and this time, it had better work or it will be the end of you, by my word!"

And Schottenhamel turned and went back into the kitchens. Our friends started to think hard: if they didn't want to incur the innkeeper's rage, they would have to figure out a way to make this blasted light travel faster to the back of the room, no matter what.

Maja, who had let herself be distracted by the open door, suddenly exclaimed, "Look at this athlete, Albert!"

A midget thrower could be seen standing on a platform. A sign read: "Niels Bohr, midget thrower, qualified by the University of Copenhagen." Making no visible effort, the giant, also third-time champion of the inter-villages cow-carrying competition of Schleswig-Holstein, tossed his partner into a sandbox on the other side of the stage, to the cheers of the onlookers. Niels Bohr had also achieved fame by an evening show in which he launched lantern-decked midgets in every direction. Folks came from all over the kingdom to the Oktoberfest to admire this fiery rocket show.

With a twinkle in his eye, Albert asked Maja, "Would you like me to send you flying across the barn?" "Not at all," Maja protested, a bit offended, "but look how he works up the momentum to give a boost to his throw!" "You're right!" admitted Albert. "To make an object go faster, it needs momentum. I would like to try the same method with a dumpling... Aim it at Heinrich's head who is over there sleeping like a log!"

Putting his words into action, Albert grabbed some potato dumplings off the tray of a comely barmaid passing by and mercilessly bombarded the poor dog, to the customers' great amusement. A round of loud applause rang out for, in those times, the Oktoberfest visitors had a highly-developed sense of humor.

"It took exactly two seconds for the dumplings to reach Heinrich," Albert observed, checking his watch.

At first a bit cross at this brutal awakening, Heinrich soon welcomed the manna falling from heaven.

"Albert," cried Maja, taken aback, "do you really think this is the right moment to be goofing off?"
"Wait, I'm not done! If I build up momentum, the dumpling will go faster and arrive sooner. Or if I do not build any momentum and it is Heinrich that runs towards me, the result would be the same, don't you agree? Since he has seen us, let's toss him another Knödel."

At the precise instant when Albert slung the bait, the dog jumped forward to catch it with a joyful yelp and this time, the Knödel only took one second to reach him.

"In other words, from Heinrich's point of view, the dumpling seemed to travel twice as fast, as it took only half the time to get from my hand to his mouth."
"Well, wouldn't it be the same with light?" replied Maja. "Imagine that a ray of light was constituted of a multitude of little specks projected forward, like so many little midgets each carrying a tiny lantern. Perhaps we could take inspiration from the athlete Niels and give them a boost so that they get to their destination faster? Ideally, we would need a giant catapult..."

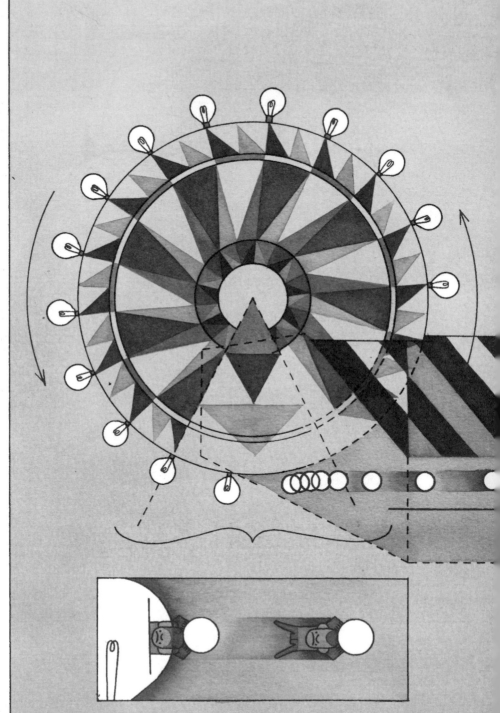

Struck with the same idea, Maja and Albert turned around together and looked at the Ferris wheel next to the marquee. Then they took off in a rush to ask the giant Niels for help. He was taking a break and was eager to lend a hand to scientific progress. With much grunting and groaning, he managed to yank the Ferris wheel from its foundations and push it all the way into Schottenhamel's marquee.

"If we wrap the string of lights around the Ferris wheel and make it spin at maximum speed," they thought, "the light will be projected to the back of the room as if with a slingshot."

The Ferris wheel, being very heavy, had crushed the floor of the marquee and, being very tall, had burst through the roof. But anything was better than having the light arrive one second late!

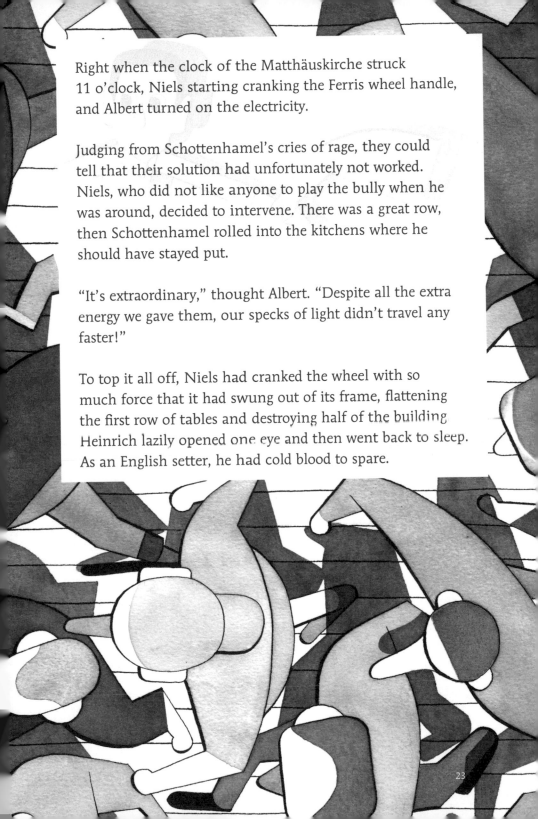

Right when the clock of the Matthäuskirche struck 11 o'clock, Niels starting cranking the Ferris wheel handle, and Albert turned on the electricity.

Judging from Schottenhamel's cries of rage, they could tell that their solution had unfortunately not worked. Niels, who did not like anyone to play the bully when he was around, decided to intervene. There was a great row, then Schottenhamel rolled into the kitchens where he should have stayed put.

"It's extraordinary," thought Albert. "Despite all the extra energy we gave them, our specks of light didn't travel any faster!"

To top it all off, Niels had cranked the wheel with so much force that it had swung out of its frame, flattening the first row of tables and destroying half of the building. Heinrich lazily opened one eye and then went back to sleep. As an English setter, he had cold blood to spare.

Albert and Maja were devastated—nothing was working out as planned! Noticing their distress, a little man stood up from his bench and came over to introduce himself:

"My dear children, my name is Abraham Michelson, and I think I understand your predicament. You might be interested to know that a few years ago, I had managed to perfect an experiment rather similar to yours, with the exception of… these minor collateral damages. It taught me that light always travels at the same speed, even if we try to move towards it to speed up the process. And so, your attempts seem hopeless to me… I am very sorry to dash your hopes but, if it is any consolation, I was never able to discover why it works this way. Do you know that, in order to measure the speed of light, Galileo had his assistants pace throughout the countryside night after night carrying lanterns? But I have invented a little device with a turning mirror that I think is quite clever… Come have a seat at my table!"

"Alas! Mr. Michelson," Maja replied, thinking him crazy, "many thanks but this is not the right moment. If we don't figure out a solution for Mister Schottenhamel, we're doomed!"

Michelson did not insist. It is said that he died in a deep crater in California, many years later, still working on measuring the speed of light with ever greater precision.

Why can we make a Knödel go faster and not a ray of light? Such is the unfathomable mystery from which modern physics would arise.

"What does the dumpling have that light doesn't, except pieces of potato?" asked Maja, perplexed.
"If I could throw midgets faster than the speed of light, what a great publicity stunt that would be!" Niels declared enthusiastically.
"Well, the best thing would be to try again!" exclaimed Albert.
"Heinrich, come here, boy! Good 'ole dog, we would like to know what happens from your perspective when we throw you a Knödel as fast as possible."

At the prospect of another serving, Heinrich's eyes lit up. Niels the athlete hadn't grasped much beyond understanding that he was supposed to throw a Knödel with all his strength. So he went to the restaurant entrance to get ready while Maja prepared herself by climbing onto Heinrich's back in order to track the Knödel's flight with her stopwatch. As for Albert, he posted himself at the approximate location where the contact was expected to occur.

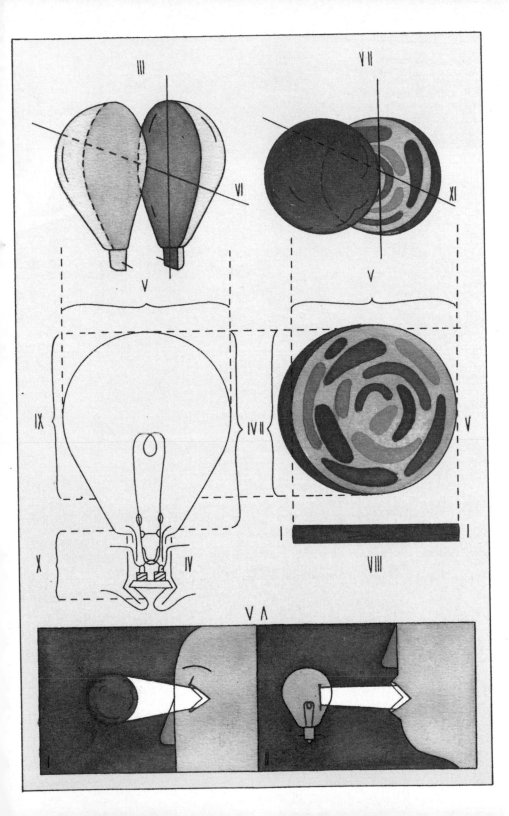

At the designated time, Niels went into action and sent the Knödel flying with incredible force. In perfect synchrony, the brother and sister started their stopwatches. As for our four-footed friend, he took off like a rocket. According to Albert's timing, he lunged forward at a rate of approximately two hundred and eighty thousand kilometers per second. He really must have been starving.

As Heinrich snapped up his reward, Albert and Maja stopped
their watches and compared the results: "How surprising,"
noted Albert. "Our watches don't show the same duration!
Maja, yours shows three-tenths of a second less than mine
does! And yet I am sure that we started timing at the same
instant. Mother made us study music theory, and she always
told us that we had an impeccable sense of rhythm."
"You mean to say that my time went by slower than yours?"
asked Maja incredulously.
"And why not? After all, what do we know about time?"
"We must be among the very first to reach such speed, and so
humanity's experiments up to now are of absolutely no help,"
concluded Niels, who was capable of waxing philosophical
from time to time.

Albert and Maja repeated the experiment over and over, allowing Niels to continue demonstrating his strength. It became increasingly harder for Heinrich to catch his reward in mid-air, either because he was full or because the throws were too violent. But when he managed to make it, the result was always the same.

All the customers had fled a long time ago, afraid of being hit by a wayward Knödel. Our friends, overexcited, observed for the first time in history that time was perhaps composed of relative dimensions.

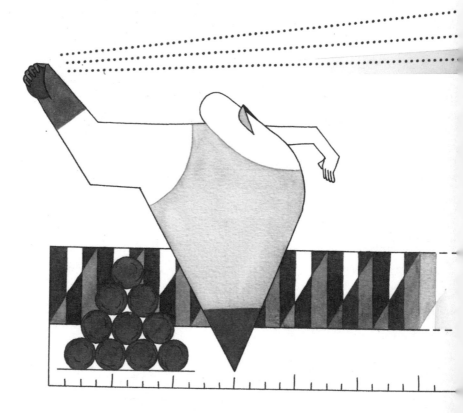

"What a shame that Mr. Michelson is no longer here!" Albert moaned. "I think I found the explanation for his experiment: If light always seems to travel at the same speed, regardless of our movement in relation to it, this is because time varies from our point of view! As we get closer to the source of light, its apparent speed should increase... but our time expands and exactly compensates for the phenomenon!"

"My friends," interrupted Niels, "all this is very interesting, but I have to prepare for my evening show, see you later!"

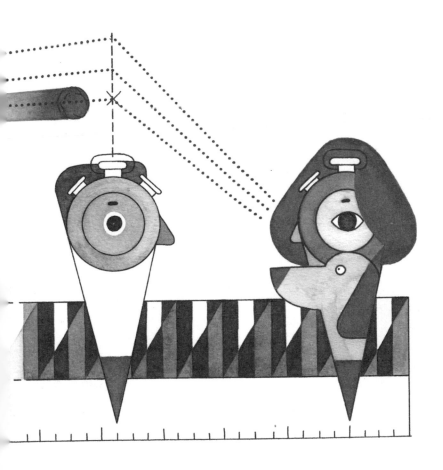

Niels had barely turned on his heel when a roar of rage
broke out. It was the innkeeper who, regaining consciousness,
discovered what the apprentice electricians had been up to.

Under the smashed tables, the floor was full of holes and,
in the now roofless room, the Knödel-coated walls were
threatening to collapse.

Schottenhamel, much too infuriated to appreciate the novelty
of the experiment, turned a deep shade of red. Then he started
hurling curses at Heinrich, Maja and Albert, who took off as
fast as their two feet (or four paws) could carry them.
As he dashed by, Heinrich, knowing that his appetite would
come back sooner or later, snagged a string of smoked sausages
hanging out of Schottenhamel's pocket. Without hesitating,
Schottenhamel grabbed the blunderbuss hidden behind the
bar and took off after them.

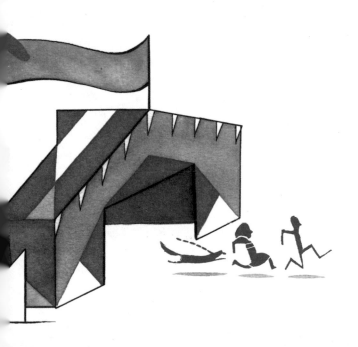

33

Our friends fled to the photographer's booth, who had been watching the commotion with enjoyment and was more than willing to quickly lend them disguises. Outside the booth, they slipped into the middle of the brass-band parade that was crossing the alley. Albert grabbed a drum, Maja a trumpet, and Heinrich took a little whistle that he found in the pocket of his suit coat; he marched proudly at the front of the procession on his hind legs. The dreadful Schottenhamel bolted past without recognizing them.

Maja, who had barely regained her composure, whispered in Albert's ear, "Why is the parade happening right now, at a quarter to noon? Wasn't it supposed to start at noon?"

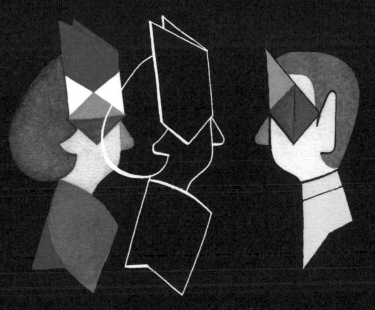

Seized by doubt, she asked the person next to her, a clarinettist who was as skinny as a rake, for the time. Seeming intensely irritated, he replied, *"Zweife, mei junga Freindin!"* which means noon in the Bavarian dialect.

"I don't understand," Maja thought to herself.
"I never saw my watch stop working or even start ticking slower."
"Maja, remember, time passed by slower from your point of view during the Knödel experiment! Consequently, you aged less. This new principle of physics promises to stir up trouble all over the place. I suggest we call it Relativity!"

Suddenly, a cry of triumph pulled them out of their reflections—it was Schottenhamel! Having backtracked, he had recognized them under their disguises and was headed straight for them. Without further ado, Albert, Maja and Heinrich took off towards the roller coasters in the hope of shaking off their pursuer.

Although a pacifist, Albert snatched a pop gun on his way past the shoot-a-pigeon stand, for the situation was becoming serious. All our friends arrived at the roller coasters right when they started to roll. Jumping into the very first car, Albert and Maja saw Heinrich leap in behind them. When Schottenhamel reached the ride, he had just enough time to hoist himself into the caboose seconds before the train took off at top speed.

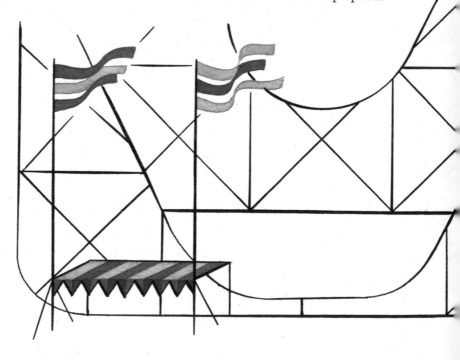

This happened to be the fastest roller coaster ever built at the time, and it was said to reach mind-boggling speeds. Incidentally, the clerks from Munich's chamber of commerce thought such a thing to be perfectly ridiculous—no one wants to be transported at such speed, and each morning as they passed by the ride with heavy steps, they shook their heads in disapproval.

Schottenhamel wasn't letting the front of the train out of his sight; he would have liked to shoot at Albert and Maja, but he only had one shot in his gun, and Heinrich with his sausages prevented him from taking proper aim. He was shouting that the dog was a thief, like all dogs for that matter, and more generally like all the people of… Munich. But Heinrich couldn't care less.

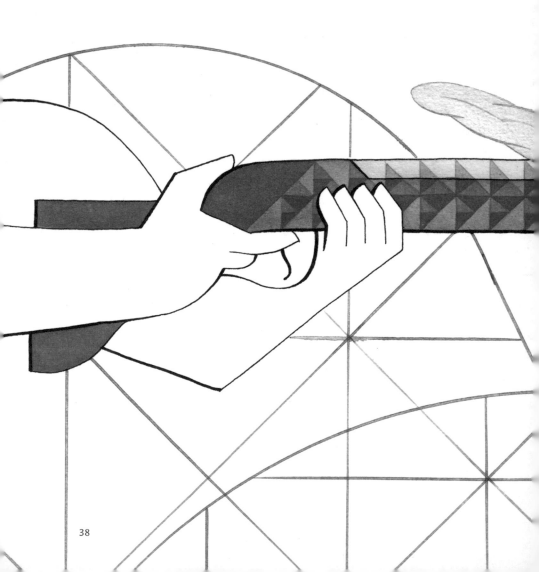

On the other hand, he didn't seem to be doing so well on the roller coaster. In the middle of a dizzying descent, he even contemplated jumping out to escape the nausea overwhelming him.

Schottenhamel, who finally had a clean shot, fired away. But Albert, quicker, had fired first. All of them, convinced of being mortally wounded, Albert, Maja and Schottenhamel let themselves fall out of the train one by one, biting the dust.

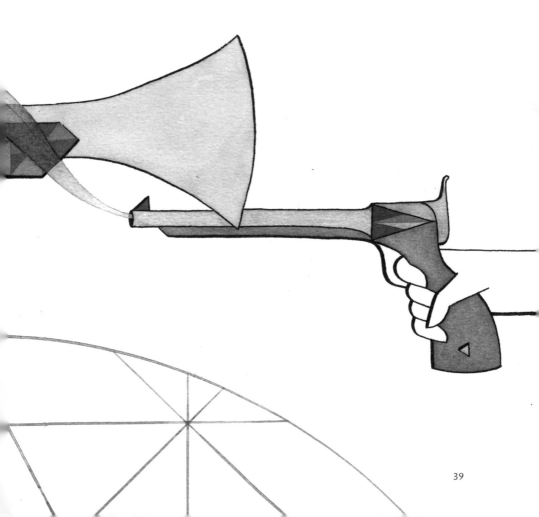

They didn't need much time to discover that they were unharmed: Albert's pistol wouldn't have hurt a fly, and it had been ages since Schottenhamel could aim straight at this late hour of the day. Jumping to their feet, our friends hastened to find refuge until the innkeeper's rage had blown over. Maja remembered that, a bit further on, she had seen a ride of steam-powered flying chairs that a gigantic reservoir of water could keep in the air "until the end of time (or almost)," as a sign promised. She hurried her brother to the ride. Albert gave all his money to the stallholder to have the maximum amount of steam power until the reservoir would be empty, and they climbed into a harness.

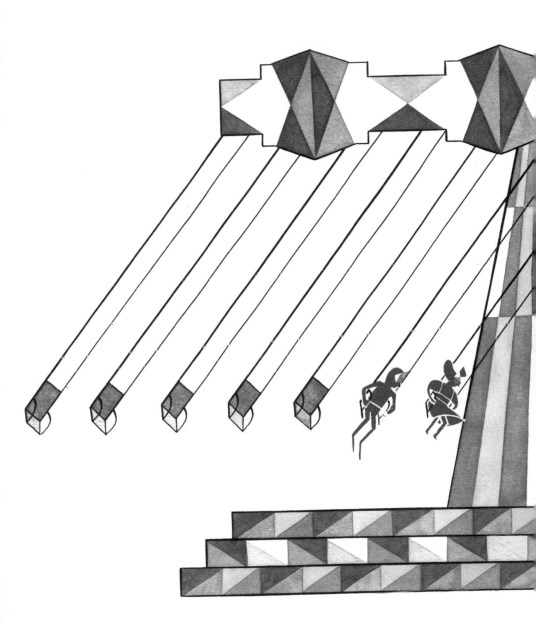

By the time Schottenhamel showed up, the extreme speed of the fairground attraction prevented anyone from coming near. Albert shuddered at the idea of spinning in circles for centuries, but then he reasoned that even the largest reservoir in the world would not be able to power a ride turning this quickly for very long!

"It would seem that it is getting harder and harder for the flying chairs to accelerate!" cried Maja whose voice was drowned out by the roar of the carousel.
"Look! We're sinking into the ground!" exclaimed Albert. "It's because of Heinrich who has eaten too many dumplings! Get off, Heinrich!"

Obediently, the poor dog unbuckled his seatbelt and was propelled several hundred meters through the air. "Boom!" he thought, bracing himself for the shock. Fortunately for him, he came in for a landing near Niels Bohr, the midget thrower, the only man capable of catching a dog flying at a speed close to the speed of light. In the meantime, the flying chairs were sinking further and further...

44

"I think the increased speed makes the carousel heavier and heavier!" Albert shouted.

Our hero's brain was churning every bit as fast as the carousel:

"Unbelievable," he thought. "Everything is happening as though the energy generated by our acceleration was converting itself into mass... And what if mass and energy were nothing but two aspects of one and the same reality? Let's calculate! If E is the energy supply and m is the supply of mass, we could imagine that E is proportional to m. They can never be directly equal, for these two measurements do not use the same units. To pass from one to the other, according to Newton, the speed squared must be added. Very well! This factor must be constant in every situation, and my constant, as I learned in the tent from Mr. Michelson, is the speed of light! If I call it c, then we can say that the energy provided by E corresponds to a rise in mass: $m = E/c^2$. Put another way, $E = mc^2$. It's simple once you figure it out!"

Maja, at her end, was simply trying not to throw up.

After five more minutes, the reservoir powering the swinging chairs was completely empty and the chairs began to slow down and then stopped with a grating noise. Albert and Maja expected to be spun around for longer than that. Very uneasy and all disheveled by their vicious race, they climbed down quickly. But Schottenhamel was nowhere to be seen.

Moreover, in the Oktoberfest alleyways, the people seemed to be wearing odd clothing, and the amusement park had started to look rather strange. They were surprised to cross several automobiles, having only seen such things in books. "Extra, extra, read the *Deutsche Allgemeine Zeitung*! Mr. Schottenhamel appointed chancellor by President Hindenburg!" hollered a newspaper seller with a postage-stamp moustache.

Albert glanced at the headline. Reading the date left him terror-stricken: they were in 1933! The terrific speed of the flying chairs had caused them to travel through time...

47

"Schottenhamel as chancellor! Do you realize what this means, Albert?" Maja asked, deeply distressed.

"The faster we go, the more our time goes by slower than other people's time," replied Albert who wasn't particularly interested in the political aspect.

"If, after the roller coaster, you hadn't climbed with me into the flying chairs, you would now be my big sister, and considerably older. How unbelievable is that?"

"But then," Maja said sadly, "what has happened to our poor Heinrich? Do you think that in moving along faster, we could go back in time and find him again?"

"Unfortunately, I doubt it. Since time stops when we reach the speed of light, I suppose we must go even faster than the speed of light in order to go back in time. Our ride was spinning full steam, yet it seemed to be limited by a maximum speed. To tell the truth, I think that reaching the speed of light would require an infinite amount of energy and so I suppose we cannot exceed it. And then imagine for a second the paradoxes that would emerge: if I go back in time, I could for example kill our father before he were to meet our mother, and thus we would not exist anymore. What a dreadful brain teaser! No, Maja, all our discoveries might appear strange, but they must not be absurd. The Creator is mysterious, but he is not malevolent!"

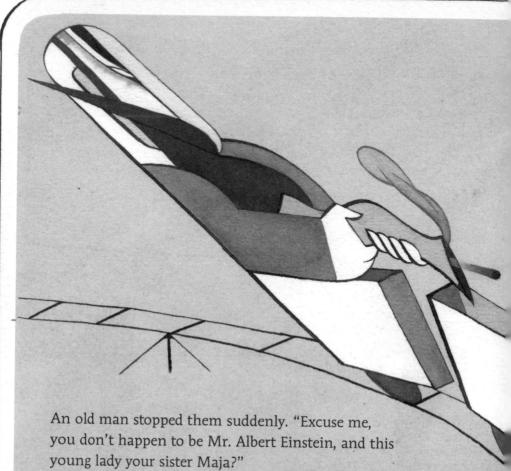

An old man stopped them suddenly. "Excuse me, you don't happen to be Mr. Albert Einstein, and this young lady your sister Maja?"

"Yes," they answered, quite surprised.

"How strange, you haven't changed a bit! And you're still wearing the disguises that I lent you thirty-seven years ago! But... you don't recognize me?"

"The photographer!" exclaimed Maja.

"Exactly! In 1896, I was already working here. I was the best photographer in Munich, maybe even in the whole of Bavaria if I may be so bold. I had the opportunity to photograph all sorts of crowned heads during my career, from the Queen of England to the Nice Carnival Queen. I happen to remember your story very well, you know . . ."

"After you passed by my booth," he continued, "I was just in the process of adjusting my cameras when you and the big Schottenhamel started shooting at each other on the roller coaster. Look at the strange photo I took at that very moment—I'll never part with it."

In the photograph, Maja, Albert, and even Schottenhamel appeared to be extremely thin. In fact, the entire train seemed to be compressed lengthwise. "When I saw this," explained the photographer, "I first told myself that my lens was flawed. But after verification, it didn't come from my equipment but from you, if I may be so bold!"

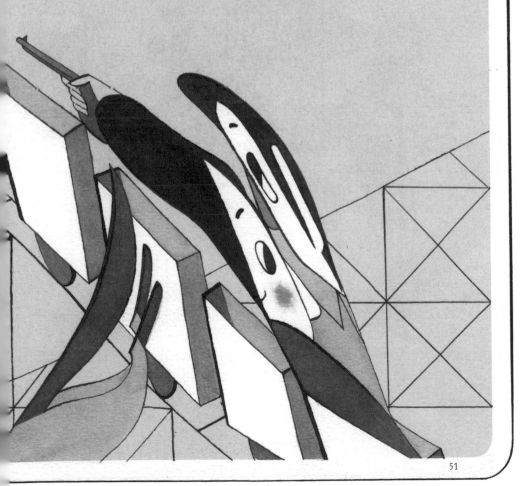

"Yet we felt no compression. It's incredible!" Maja responded. "Perhaps for us, the entire Universe contracted! Not only our outer shells, but also our bones, our muscles, our joints, and so on! Our bodily organs all retained the same relative size, each in relation to another, and thus the compression did not harm them."

"That's possible," said Albert, "but what strikes me the most is to see Heinrich fall with his collar of sausages while, at the end of the train, Schottenhamel is shooting at us while we haven't yet moved a muscle. That doesn't seem strange to you?"

"Quite so," Maja replied, "Heinrich was closer to us at the front of the train, and so the image of the jumping dog reached our eyes before it reached the eyes of our enemy! And so you had to have been the first one to shoot!"

"Do you know that Schottenhamel sued you in the courts at the time?" interjected the photographer with excitement. "Since you didn't want to come down from your devilish flying chairs, you were judged in absentia for failure to appear, if I may be so bold. Schottenhamel accused you of shooting at him first, whereas on my photo, it is clear that he was the one to take the first shot. Having lost his lawsuit, furious, he decided to go into politics!"

"This is incredible!" cried Albert. "We have the experimental and zoological confirmation that the order of events is not the same depending on the relative point of view. From the train, it seemed to us that I am the first to shoot, followed by Schottenhamel. But from our friend the photographer's point of view, the shot by Schottenhamel from the rear of the train happened first. So even while the front and the rear of the train were taken simultaneously by the photographer, for us, the front lags behind the rear. During this lapse of time, the rear moves slightly towards the front, and this is why we have the impression of seeing the train compress itself, whereas no such thing occurs. Thank God, this inversion of chronology is what allowed us to be acquitted. In this affair, the court preferred to rely upon the photograph rather than on Schottehamel's account."

"And yet Schottenhamel was telling the truth."

"He was telling his truth, which is not that of an exterior observer, my dear Maja! In our case, time, lengths and even the truth have become relative!"

Albert and Maja asked the photographer about their dog Heinrich. "If I may be so bold," he told them, "your companion must be the oldest dog in the world! After having been flung out of the flying chair ride, he was taken in by Niels Bohr and has worked with him ever since in the Palace of Mirrors!"

At these words, our two friends warmly thanked the photographer, gave him back his disguises and took off in search of their dog.

Upon arriving at the Palace of Mirrors, Albert and Maja had no trouble recognizing good 'ole Heinrich, busily enjoying a sausage. On the other hand, Niels Bohr, the retired midget thrower whose statuesque proportions had been famousin the previous century, had changed a lot. He had become considerably stooped and skinny with age. Having strained his back when he had caught Heinrich, he had had plenty of time to mull over the Knödel experiment while Albert and Maja spun around on their flying chairs. Returning to the University of Copenhagen, he studied physics for twenty years, then, nostalgic for the booths of the Oktoberfest, he had come back to Munich and purchased the old Palace of Mirrors where he had adapted his evening show of hurling lantern-lit midgets.

"Nowadays, I throw photons," he announced proudly.
"Excuse me?" asked Maja.
"Yes, photons, those little particles of light that you tried in the past to get to accelerate. As they have zero mass, it is much more convenient than throwing lantern-lit midgets! Okay, so it may not be quite as impressive, but I have built receptors that light up in multiple colors when they detect the photons passing through. You should come see it at night, it's gorgeous! Moreover, the audience participates. One must live with the times, as our moronic chancellor Schottenhamel likes to say!"

"Look how much fun it is—it's called quantum petanque because photons are quanta, or tiny quantities of energy, if you prefer. The principle is simple: for one Reichsmark, you are given ten photons to throw into the entryway of the Palace of Mirrors. Inside, they bounce around a little bit everywhere and, as the mirrors are rather old, sometimes they reflect the photons, while sometimes they let them pass through — one can never really know. At the end of their course, the photons come out through one of the lanterns you see over there. Near the exit there is a highly responsive sensor which is activated at the slightest touch of light. If, upon leaving, some photons touch this sensor, it starts vibrating and you win! You want to try?"

Albert and Maja threw several photons into the palace; the receptors lit up all over the place, but the photons come out without touching the sensor.

"How much are you willing to bet that I can activate the sensor in one try?" Niels asked with a wink. Upon speaking, he gently whistled at Heinrich, who disappeared into the Palace of Mirrors. Niels threw a series of photons with all his force and the sensor started vibrating!

"That's impossible!" cried Albert and Maja together.

"Well, well, well," puffed Niels who was obviously enjoying himself a great deal. "You know that everybody has the same reaction you are having? I'll tell you the secret: when my customers throw photons into the Palace of Mirrors, there happens to be, at the exit, a shadow zone they never reach, and that's where I install my sensor, of course. In addition, I take care to disconnect the detectors behind the mirrors so that they light up completely randomly, without any connection to the trajectory of the photons. But when I perform my demonstration, I whistle to Heinrich who enters the palace, and I reactivate the detectors. That way, this good 'ole boy can observe the exact trajectory of the photons. And whether you believe it or not, the mere fact that there exists a way of following the photons is enough to make the shadow zone disappear! The best part is that even I do not know how it works— it's as though there is a little imp inside responsible for sheer coincidence; as soon as we try to catch him, he sneaks away and takes his shadow zone with him!"

"This makes no sense to me," Albert scowled, "and I hate not understanding..."

"Some of my colleagues think that the photon exists in several parallel worlds at the same time, wherein it follows a different trajectory each time. According to them, the shadow zone comes from the coexistence of these parallel worlds and from the impossibility of knowing in which world we find ourselves, unless we engage in observation. As soon as there is an observer, the multiplicity of these worlds is reduced to a single world."

"I find this theory a bit speculative," ventured Maja.

"Imagine that, according to this theory, there exists a world in which I did not become a midget thrower, my deepest passion! In which you did not climb into the flying chairs! Albert, you would now be an old respectable man with white hair, perhaps even a Nobel prize laureate! It wouldn't be Schottenhamel who would have been chancellor, but anyone else, why, perhaps this awful Adolf character who was selling newspapers earlier! You know, I am familiar with his ideas and you would have been dead meat."

"And how many more worlds could we still imagine?
And how do these multiple worlds interact with each other?"
"God does not play dice," Albert quipped.
"But who are you, Albert Einstein,
to tell God what he must do?"

French edition

Frédéric Morlot & Anne-Margot Ramstein

Les illuminations d'Albert Einstein

Design: Yohanna Nguyen

© Les petits Platons, Paris 2011

With the kind support of

INSTITUT
FRANÇAIS

First edition

ISBN 978-3-03734-935-9

© diaphanes, Zurich-Berlin 2017

www.platoandco.net

www.diaphanes.com

Layout: 2edit, Zurich

Printed and bound in Germany

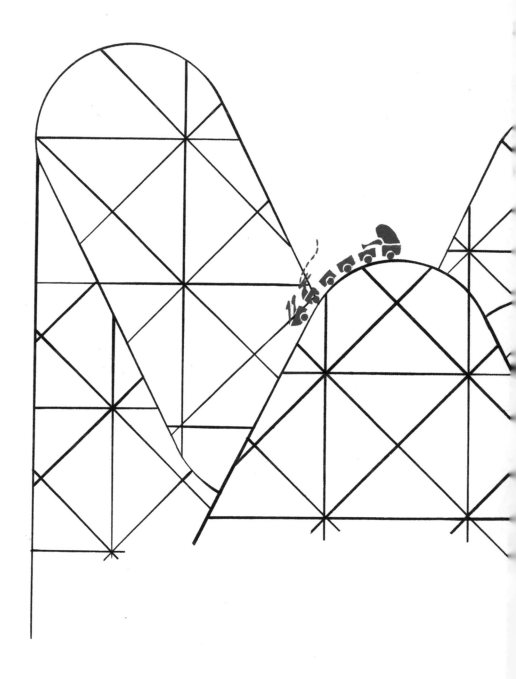